CAROLING

CONTENTS

First published 1990 by
The Hamlyn Publishing Group, Michelin House,
81 Fulham Road, London SW3 6RB, England

© Copyright illustrations Caroline and John Astrop 1990
© Copyright text The Hamlyn Publishing Group, a division of
The Octopus Publishing Group Limited 1990

ISBN 0 600 56391 X
Printed in Czechoslovakia

50506

CAROLINE AND JOHN ASTROP'S

FAVOURITE FAIRY TALES

HAMLYN

Cinderella

Cinderella was crying. She was very miserable. "Here I am, sitting by the kitchen fire in my rags," she thought, "and my ugly sisters have gone to the ball. Oh, how I wish I could have a beautiful dress and go to the ball, too."

Poor Cinderella had a very hard life. Her sisters made her work all day scrubbing floors, and doing all the housework and washing. They were very jealous of Cinderella because she was much prettier than they were. They were so jealous that they made Cinderella stay at home while they went to the ball at the King's palace.

"Oh dear, how unhappy I am," Cinderella wept.

"Why are you weeping, my dear?"

Suddenly, from out of nowhere, Cinderella heard a voice. She looked up and there, standing in front of her, was a beautiful lady. She wore a lovely dress and carried a wand in her hand.

"Why are you crying?" the lady asked again.

"Because I cannot go to the ball," Cinderella replied.

"Oh, but you can!" the lady told her.

"I am your fairy godmother. I can make wonderful things happen. Look at this!"

The fairy godmother waved her wand over a large pumpkin. At once, it turned into a fine coach. Cinderella gasped with surprise.

"The coach must have horses," said the fairy godmother, "and you need a jolly fat coachman to drive it."

She waved her wand over six mice and a big fat rat. At once, the mice became six beautiful horses. The rat turned into a coachman in a fine velvet suit.

"But I have no clothes to wear!" Cinderella protested. "How can I go to the ball in these rags?"

"We'll soon see about that!" the fairy godmother told her. She gave another wave of her wand. All at once, Cinderella's rags turned into a lovely silk and lace ball gown. She looked down and saw that there were dainty glass slippers on her feet.

"Oh thank you, thank you!" Cinderella cried. "I am so happy. Now I can go to the ball!"

"Indeed you can," said the fairy godmother. "But be sure to leave by midnight. The magic does not last any later than that!"

When Cinderella arrived at the ball in her fine coach and lovely dress, everyone turned to stare at her. The prince, the King's son, was wonderstruck.

"Who is this beautiful girl?" he wanted to know. "How graceful she is. I must dance with her."

Cinderella and the prince danced the whole evening. In fact, the prince danced with no one else. Cinderella's ugly sisters were furious. They wanted the prince to pay attention to them. They did not know that the girl was their sister Cinderella, because they had never seen her so beautifully dressed before.

"I have fallen in love with you," the prince told Cinderella, as they whirled around the dance floor. "Will you marry me?"

Cinderella was very happy to hear this, because she had fallen in love with the prince, too. But before she could reply, the clock began to strike.

"Oh dear, it cannot be midnight already," she thought in alarm.

But it WAS midnight. Cinderella had enjoyed herself so much that she had not noticed the hours passing by.

In a great fright, Cinderella ran from the ballroom.

She was just running down the palace steps when the clock struck midnight. At once, her beautiful dress turned to rags. The coach became a pumpkin again. The horses and coachman turned into six mice and a rat once more. The only things left were Cinderella's glass slippers. In her rush to get away, she left one of them on the palace steps. The other slipper was still on her

foot when she reached home. She hid it away so that her ugly sisters would not find it.

The prince was very unhappy when Cinderella disappeared. All he had was a glass slipper which a guard had found on the steps. Then, the prince had an idea.

"I can use this slipper to find her," he decided. "The girl whose foot fits the slipper will be the girl I danced with at the ball. And that is the girl I will marry!"

So, next day, the King ordered that every girl in the land must try on the glass slipper. The slipper was placed on a velvet cushion and the King's servants carried it to every town and village and every house in the land. Every girl wanted to try it on, because every girl wanted to marry the prince. Princesses tried the slipper on. So did duchesses and fine ladies. But the slipper was far too small for any of them.

Then, one day, the King's servants brought the glass slipper to the house where Cinderella and her sisters lived. The sisters tried it on first. They pushed and shoved and pushed again, but the slipper did not fit either of them.

"It is Cinderella's turn to try the slipper now," said the King's servants.

"Cinderella!" laughed the ugly sisters. "Why she was not at the prince's ball! How can the slipper belong to her? Don't be silly!"

"Our orders are that every girl in the land must try on the slipper," the servants said.

Of course, when Cinderella put her foot into the glass slipper, it fitted perfectly. The servants were very pleased.

"This is the beautiful girl our prince is looking for!" they cried.

"Nonsense!" the ugly sisters said crossly. "It cannot be!"

"Oh yes it can!" replied the fairy godmother. She had appeared again. She waved her wand and at once Cinderella's rags were changed into the lovely gown she had worn at the ball.

"Now, Cinderella, fetch the other glass slipper which you hid away," said the fairy godmother. "Your prince is waiting for you!"

The prince was very happy to see Cinderella again and that very same day, they were married.

The King was happy, too, and so was the Queen, the prince's mother. In fact, everyone in the land was happy because the prince had married such a beautiful girl. Everyone, that is, except for Cinderella's ugly, jealous sisters.

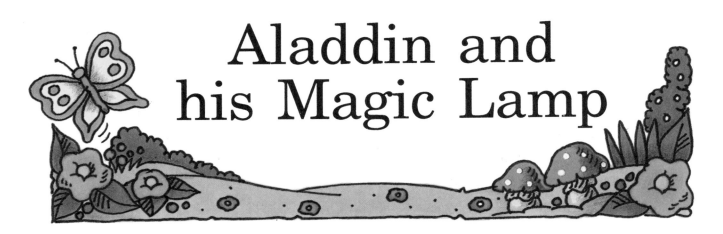

Aladdin and
his Magic Lamp

One day a wizard came to the little town where Aladdin lived with his poor widowed mother.

The wizard was looking for a young lad to do some work for him.

"He must not be too tall, and certainly not too fat," said the wizard. "And he must be strong!"

When he saw Aladdin, he said:

"This boy will do very nicely!"

He called to him. "Hey, you lad – come over here! If you come with me, I can show you where you can find gold and jewels and all kinds of treasure!"

Aladdin said "Yes" straight away. He and his mother were very poor, so the thought of being rich was very exciting.

The wizard took Aladdin a long way away from the town where he lived.

"Here we are!" said the wizard.

Aladdin was puzzled. All he could see was rock and sand for miles around.

The wizard waved his hands in the air and chanted a magic spell. At once, a big cave opened up in the ground. It was very deep and very dark.

"There is treasure and gold down there," the wizard told Aladdin. "You can have all of it. What I want is the lamp you will find in the cave. Take this magic ring – it will help you find your way in."

Aladdin had to squeeze and push hard to get into the cave, but at last he managed it.

"There is the lamp," he said, and he took it from the cave wall and hung it around his neck.

Then, he looked about for the gold and jewels. He could not see any.

Suddenly, everything went dark.

"The cave has closed up again," thought Aladdin in alarm. "I'm trapped."

High above, in the desert, the wizard tried all sorts of spells to open the cave again. But his magic was not strong enough. The cave stayed shut, with Aladdin inside.

"Oooooh, stuff!" muttered the wizard. "Now I have to go home with nothing!"

Aladdin sat in the dark wondering what to do. Then he remembered the wizard's ring, which was on his finger.

"Maybe the ring can help me!" he said.

He twisted it round on his finger and the cave opened again. Aladdin squeezed out and went home.

Aladdin's mother was glad to see him safe. But she was sorry that there was no treasure, only the lamp which Aladdin had hung around his neck.

"Oh, well," she said. "I can polish it and use it to light the house."

Aladdin's mother started rubbing the lamp to make it shine. Suddenly, there was a flash and a bang and a huge genie came out of the lamp in a cloud of blue smoke. "I am the slave of the lamp!" the genie said in a loud voice. "What is your wish, master?"

16

"My wish? Oh, goodness!" For a moment, Aladdin was so surprised he could not think what to say. "Er, bring us a huge meal!"

Flash! Bang! The genie pointed his finger and wonderful, tasty food appeared from nowhere.

"Bring us gold and jewels!" Aladdin cried.

Flash! Bang! Flash! Gold and jewels appeared.

"We're rich!" Aladdin shouted joyfully. "We can have anything we want from now on!"

One day, a beautiful princess came to the town. As soon as Aladdin saw her, he fell in love with her.

"Her father, the Sultan, is very rich," he thought. "He will let me marry her if I can show him I am even richer than he is. This is a job for the genie!"

Aladdin summoned the genie and told him to build a magnificent palace for him. It was much richer than the Sultan's palace. When he saw it, the Sultan agreed to let Aladdin marry his daughter.

So, Aladdin became a prince and he and his princess lived very happily together. Then, one day, the wizard heard about the wonderful palace and came to see it. He realized that the prince who owned it was the very same Aladdin he had left behind in the cave.

"He must have the lamp!" the wizard thought. "I must get it from him!"

So, the wizard disguised himself as a pedlar. He hung a tray of new lamps around his neck and went round the town calling: "New lamps for old! New lamps for old!"

18

The princess, of course, did not know that Aladdin's lamp was magic. The wizard was delighted when the princess gave it to him and in its place took a new lamp which was not magic at all.

As soon as he got his hands on it, the wizard summoned the genie out of the lamp.

"Take me, Aladdin's palace and his princess to Africa!" the wizard commanded. The genie obeyed.

Flash! Bang! The palace disappeared.

Aladdin was terribly upset when he found his palace, his wife and treasures gone.

"I still have the wizard's ring, though!" he said. "Maybe that will help me."

Aladdin twisted the ring on his finger. At once, he found himself at the palace in Africa.

The princess was very happy to see him.

"We must get hold of the magic lamp!" Aladdin told her. "Only the genie can save us. I have a plan – listen!"

Aladdin hid himself in the wizard's room where the lamp was kept. The wizard was sitting at the table admiring the lamp, when suddenly he heard the princess cry out.

"Wizard! Wizard! Come quickly!" she called. "Thieves are stealing your gold!"

The wizard jumped up in a fright. Forgetting about the lamp for a moment, he rushed out to catch the thieves and save his gold.

Aladdin jumped from his hiding place and grabbed the lamp. He rubbed it and the genie appeared.

"Make the wizard disappear for ever!" he commanded.

"I obey, master!" said the genie.

With a flash and a bang, the wizard vanished and was never seen again. After that, the genie took Aladdin and his princess and his palace back to their own land.

"I will never give the lamp away again," the princess promised Aladdin. "The genie is our best friend!"

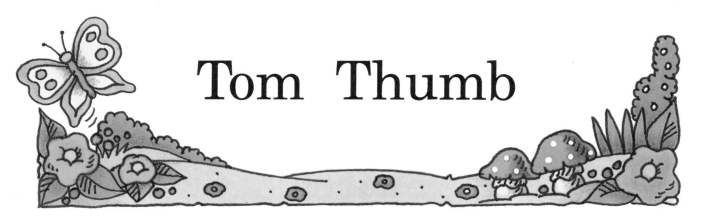

Tom Thumb

Tom Thumb was the smallest little boy in the whole world. He was so small that he was only as tall as his father's thumb. And that was how he got such a suitable name.

"He is very tiny," said his father and his mother. "But he is our only son, and we love him very much."

Little Tom loved his parents in return and tried to help them in any way he could.

One day, his father, who was a peasant, was going into the forest to cut some wood.

"I would like to take my horse and cart to the forest clearing to carry back the wood," Tom's father said. "But there is no one to drive the cart..."

"I'll do it, father!" Tom offered. "I'll sit by the horse's ear and tell it where to go."

"What a good idea!" said Tom's father.

The horse and cart set off into the forest and Tom spoke into the horse's ear, telling it which path to take to get to the forest clearing. As the cart was travelling along, two men saw it and thought it was moving without a driver.

"That's strange!" said one man to the other. "Let's follow it and see where it is going."

At last, the horse and cart reached the clearing where Tom's father was cutting wood. The two men, following behind, were amazed to see him take Tom from the horse's ear and put him down on a log.

"Good gracious! Look how tiny he is!" the two men said. "Look, my man," they said to Tom's father. "We would like to buy your little boy and put him in a circus. He could earn lots of money."

"Sell my little Tom Thumb?" the father exclaimed. "Never! He is my son and I love him."

Then, Tom jumped up and standing on his father's collar, whispered into his ear. "Take the money, father. I can easily escape and come back to you and mother."

"What a good idea!" Tom's father agreed.

So, he took the hundred gold coins the men offered him for Tom. Tom jumped on the brim of one man's hat and waved his father goodbye.

The two men walked through the forest until it became dark. Tom waited until they sat down to eat their supper. Then, when they were not looking, he crept away and hid in a mousehole.

"Goodbye to you!" Tom called cheekily to the two men. "The circus will have to do without me!"

The two men were furious when they found that Tom was gone. Following the sound of his voice, they poked sticks down the mousehole, trying to reach him. But Tom escaped. He crawled away down the mousehole and came back up to the surface a long way off.

As he crawled out of the hole, Tom heard two robbers talking.

"The squire has a lot of gold," said one robber.

"How are we going to get our hands on it?" said the other.

"I can tell you how!" a little voice told them. It was Tom. The robbers jumped with fright.

"Who's that?" they cried. They looked about on the ground and saw Tom.

"I can help you," Tom told them. "I'm small enough to squeeze through the bars of the squire's window. Then I'll pass the gold to you."

The robbers agreed to Tom's plan, but as soon as he squeezed through the window bars, he started shouting: "Robbers! Thieves! They're stealing the gold! Robbers!"

Tom made such a noise that the squire's servants woke up. They seized hold of the robbers and took them to the police.

By this time, Tom was very tired. He came to a barn and fell asleep in the warm hay. The next thing he knew, he was moving around inside a cow's mouth. The milkmaid had come to feed the cows and had given them the hay where Tom lay asleep. Before Tom could save himself, the cow had swallowed him.

Tom jumped up and down inside the cow's stomach, shouting and yelling. "Help! Help!" he cried as loudly as he could.

The milkmaid got a terrible shock. She did not know about Tom. She thought the cow was talking. She ran to fetch the squire.

The squire listened to Tom shouting and said:

"Quick, give the cow a hard slap on the back." The cow hiccupped loudly, and much to the amazement of the squire and the milkmaid, out popped Tom. Before

they could ask him how he got there, though, a fox
came by. The fox saw Tom and darted into the barn.
Before anyone could stop it, the fox grabbed Tom and
gobbled him up.

"Oh dear, first a cow, now a fox!" thought Tom, as he
sat inside the fox's stomach. Then, Tom thought of a
plan.

"Hey, fox," he called. "Are you hungry?"

The fox stopped running through the forest and looked
around to find the strange voice.

"Who's there?" the fox called nervously.

"It's me — Tom!" the voice replied. "I'm in your
stomach! You swallowed me — remember?"

"Of course I remember," the fox told Tom crossly.

"I said — are you hungry?"

"I am always hungry," grumbled the fox.

"I know where you can find food," Tom said. "Lots of lovely food . . . just go where I tell you."

Tom told the fox which paths to follow through the forest. The fox did not know it, but Tom was guiding him to the house where his mother and father lived. As soon as the fox got there, Tom started shouting.

"Father! Father!" he yelled. "I'm inside the fox — get me out, quick!"

Tom's father was surprised to hear his son's voice, but he grabbed a long wooden spoon, dipped deep down into the surprised fox's throat and pulled out his son. The frightened fox ran off as fast as his legs would carry him.

"Oh father!" Tom cried. "I am so glad to see you. What adventures I have had! Wait until I tell you where I have been — you won't believe it!"

When Tom told his father all that had happened to him, he DID believe him. A lot of things can happen to a boy the size of a thumb, that cannot happen to ordinary boys.

Snow White and the Seven Dwarfs

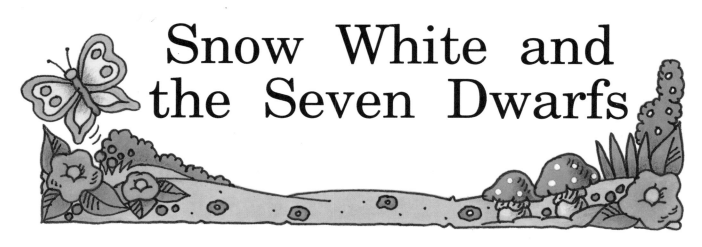

Every day, the Queen looked into her magic mirror. She knew she was beautiful. No one, she was sure, could be as beautiful as she was.

"Mirror, mirror on the wall," she said. "Who is the fairest one of all?"

And every day, the mirror answered: "You, oh Queen, are the fairest one of all!"

Then, one day, the Queen asked the mirror the same question, but she got a different answer.

"You, oh Queen, are fair 'tis true," said the mirror. "But Snow White is far fairer than you."

"Snow White!" the Queen shrieked.

Snow White was the Queen's stepdaughter. She was indeed beautiful.

The Queen was very angry. She knew the mirror always told the truth.

"I must get rid of Snow White," she decided. "Then I can be the fairest once again."

The Queen summoned one of the royal huntsmen. "Take Snow White into the forest and kill her!" she commanded.

But the huntsman could not bear to harm such a beautiful girl. Instead of killing Snow White, he let her go and, leaving her in the forest, he rode back to the palace.

Snow White was frightened when she found herself alone in the forest. She was also hungry and wandered along searching for food. Then, she saw a cottage. The front door was open, so she went in.

"My goodness!" cried Snow White. "There are seven of

everything in here. Seven chairs round the fire. Seven knives and forks and cups and saucers on the table. I wonder who lives here?"

Snow White found some food, but after eating it she felt very tired. So she went upstairs and lay down to sleep on one of the seven beds she found up there.

A little while later, the men who owned the cottage came home from work. There were seven of them and they were all dwarfs. The dwarfs worked in the gold and diamond mines in the mountains. When they found Snow White asleep, they were surprised, but pleased.

"She is a lovely girl," they said. "Maybe she will stay and look after us?"

When Snow White woke up, she was frightened to see seven strange faces staring down at her. But she soon realized the dwarfs were very kind and she agreed to stay with them.

Back at the palace, the Queen was looking in her mirror once again.

"Snow White is dead," she said. She did not know that the huntsman had left the girl in the forest. "So I am again the fairest one of all."

But when she asked the mirror the question, she did not like the answer.

"You, oh Queen are fair, 'tis true," the mirror told her. "But Snow White, who lives with the seven dwarfs, is far fairer than you!"

"Snow White is alive!" the Queen shrieked, in a rage. "But not for long. I will go and kill her myself!"

The Queen disguised herself as a poor pedlar. She put some pretty trinkets on a tray. Among them was a poisoned comb. Then, she went to the dwarfs' cottage and knocked on the door.

"Who's there?" Snow White called.

"A poor woman with pretty things to sell," the Queen replied.

Snow White opened the door. As she bent her head to look at the trinkets on the tray, the wicked Queen stuck the poisoned comb in her hair. At once, Snow White fainted and fell to the floor.

The dwarfs got a terrible shock when they came home and found Snow White. The poisoned comb was still in her hair. They took it out and to their relief, Snow White opened her eyes.

When she told the dwarfs what had happened, they said: "The wicked Queen has done this! Everyone knows she is jealous of you, Snow White."

When the Queen returned home, she went straight to her mirror.

"Who is the fairest one of all?" she demanded.

"Snow White, who lives with the seven dwarfs," the mirror replied.

The Queen screamed with fury. Once again, she planned how she would kill Snow White.

"This time I will not fail!" she muttered.

Next day, a village girl called at the dwarfs' cottage. "Lovely apples!" she cried. "Lovely apples for sale!"

"Go away!" Snow White told her. "I don't want any apples!"

After the fright over the poisoned comb, Snow White was afraid to open the door in case the wicked Queen called again. The village girl WAS the Queen, of course, wearing another disguise.

"What is the matter, dear?" the Queen asked. "Are you afraid the apples are poisoned? They are not. Look, I will bite one myself."

The Queen picked out an apple which had one side green and one side red. She took a bite out of the green half.

"There, you see!" she said.

"I suppose it is all right," Snow White thought. She took the apple and bit a piece out of the red side. At once, she fell down in a faint. The red side of the apple had been poisoned.

"Now, mirror," said the Queen when she reached the palace. "Who is the fairest one of all?"

"You are, oh Queen," the mirror replied.

"At last, Snow White is dead!" the Queen cried.

Snow White looked as if she were dead. The dwarfs could not wake her up, however hard they tried. So, sorrowfully, they put her in a glass casket. They stood round it, looking at her and all seven cried bitterly.

One day, a handsome prince came riding by. He saw Snow White in her glass casket and the dwarfs crying over her.

"What has happened?" the prince wanted to know. "Surely this lovely girl cannot be dead!"

"She is! Oh, she is!" sobbed the dwarfs and told the prince what had occurred.

"Let me take Snow White back to my palace," said the prince. "I have fallen in love with her."

Sadly, the dwarfs agreed. The prince ordered his servants to lift the glass casket and place it on a carriage. As the servants lifted the casket, a piece of poisoned apple fell out of Snow White's mouth. At once, she opened her eyes and sat up.

The prince was overjoyed. The dwarfs cheered and cheered. "Snow White is alive!" they cried. "She has come back to us!"

There and then, the prince asked Snow White to marry him. She said "Yes" at once.

So, the prince took Snow White to his own land far away and there they were married. All seven of the dwarfs came to the wedding, of course.

A little while later, the wicked Queen again asked her magic mirror: "Who is the fairest one of all?"

"Snow White, the prince's bride," came the answer.

In a rage the Queen rushed to the cottage in the forest, but it was empty. Snow White was far, far away, where the Queen could not find her. So Snow White, not the Queen, would always be the fairest one of all.

Jack and the Beanstalk

J ack cried, as he stared out of his bedroom window:
"Gosh, that wasn't there last night! Where on
earth did it come from?"

There was a huge beanstalk growing outside the
cottage where Jack lived with his widowed mother. It
was so tall that the top disappeared into the clouds
hundreds of feet above.

"It must have grown during the night while
I was asleep," thought Jack.
"But how?" he wondered.

Then Jack remembered. The
beanstalk was growing on the
spot where his mother had
thrown some beans out
of the window the
day before. Jack's
mother had been
very angry about
those beans.

"I send you to market to sell the cow," she shouted at Jack. "We need the money. Yet, you come back with a bag of worthless beans. What can you buy with beans?"

Jack tried to explain that he had met a tinker on the road to the market. The man offered the beans in exchange for the cow. But his mother was too angry to listen. She threw the beans out of the window and sent Jack to bed without his supper.

Now, this huge beanstalk was growing where the beans had landed on the ground.

"I wonder what's at the top?" Jack said. "I must find out!"

The climb up the beanstalk took many hours, but at last Jack reached the top. He looked around him. There was a whole new land here in the sky. It was like a desert with rocks and stones lying all over the ground.

Then, Jack saw a big castle a short distance away. "At least someone lives here!" he said. Feeling hopeful, he started walking. As he approached the castle, he saw a very tall woman standing by the door.

"Who are you?" she wanted to know.

Jack gulped. He felt a bit afraid. "I'm Jack," he said in a small voice. "I'm hungry! Could you give me some bread, please?"

To his relief, the woman replied:

"Oh, you poor thing! Of course you can have some bread, and I've got cheese and milk, too!"

Jack had eaten no breakfast, so he was glad to have the food the woman gave him. Then, just as he was eating, he heard a terrible thump-thump-thumping noise. The whole room shook and the cups and saucers began to clatter on the table.

The woman looked frightened. "Oh, goodness, it's my husband!" she cried. "He eats little boys like you, Jack! Quick – hide in the oven!"

Jack did as he was told. The woman quickly closed the oven door. Then, as Jack peeped through a chink in the door, he saw the woman's husband come in. He was a giant, tall as a house, with enormous hands and a big ugly face.

"Fee, fi, fo, fum, I smell the blood of an Englishman!" the giant roared.

"Oh, nonsense, dear," his wife told him. "There are no Englishmen here! Come on now, I have made you a nice supper."

Jack held his breath. Would the giant come looking for him?

Then Jack gave a sigh of relief. The giant was eating his supper.

"Bring me the goose that lays the golden eggs," he told his wife when he had finished.

The woman brought the goose and put it on the table. "Lay an egg!" the giant demanded.

At once, the goose laid a shiny golden egg. Jack's eyes opened wide as he watched. At the giant's command, the goose laid another golden egg, then another and another.

At last, the giant began to yawn. His eyes closed and he fell asleep. Jack listened to the giant snoring for many minutes before he pushed open the oven door.

Jack moved quickly. He snatched the goose off the table and ran out of the castle. He kept on running until he reached the beanstalk, then scrambled down it as fast as he could.

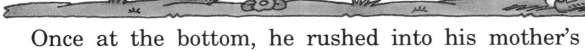

Once at the bottom, he rushed into his mother's kitchen. "Look at this, mother!" he said.

Jack put the goose on the table and told it to lay an egg. At once, a golden egg appeared on the table.

Jack's mother could hardly believe her eyes. When Jack sold the golden eggs, he and his mother became very rich. After a time, Jack began to think about climbing the beanstalk again.

"The giant must have other treasures," he said. "I must find out."

In fact, Jack went back up the beanstalk twice more. The second time, he came back safely with the giant's great moneybags of gold and silver. The third time, though, things went wrong and Jack was in great danger.

This third time, Jack hid in the wash tub when the giant came in for his supper. Afterwards, the giant called for his golden harp. The harp was a wonderful treasure. At the giant's command, it played beautiful music. Before long, the music sent the giant to sleep. Jack crept out of the tub and grabbed the harp. Then to his alarm, the harp began to cry out:

"Master! Master! Save me!"

At this, the giant woke up. He was just in time to see Jack running out of the door carrying the harp. With a mighty roar, the giant chased after him.

Jack had never run so fast in all his life. He slid down the beanstalk in a great rush. As he reached the ground, he yelled out: "Mother! Quick! Fetch an axe!"

Jack could see the giant high above, climbing down the beanstalk. Quickly, he swung the axe. The blade went straight through the beanstalk. It toppled over. The giant began to fall and landed with a tremendous crash. He was dead.

Now, Jack and his mother were very rich indeed. The goose laid golden eggs whenever they wanted. There was plenty of gold and silver in the moneybags. And whenever they wanted to hear beautiful music, the harp was there to play it for them.

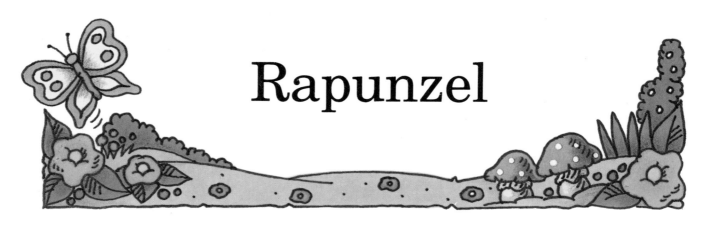

Rapunzel

Rapunzel was a beautiful girl. She lived with a wicked witch who was very jealous of her. "I don't want anyone to see her," said the witch. "She is so beautiful that men will fall in love with her straight away and want to marry her."

So, the witch locked Rapunzel away in a high tower, deep in the forest. The tower had no front door and no stairs. There was only a tiny window at the top, in the room where Rapunzel lived. When the witch wanted to get into the tower, she called out:

"Rapunzel! Rapunzel! Let down your hair!"

Rapunzel had beautiful long golden hair. It was so long that it reached all the way to the ground. When the witch called to her, Rapunzel let down her hair and the witch climbed up it to get into the tower.

One day, a handsome prince came riding through the forest. He saw the tower and thought it was rather strange.

"What is it doing here, in the middle of the forest?" he wondered.

Just then, the witch came back from gathering berries in the forest. "Rapunzel! Rapunzel! Let down your hair!"

the witch called out.

The prince watched in amazement as the witch climbed up the hair into the tower. The prince also saw Rapunzel at the window.

"How beautiful she is!" he said. "I must get into the tower to meet her."

So, the prince waited until the witch left the tower again. Then, he went to the foot of the tower and called out: "Rapunzel! Rapunzel! Let down your hair!"

When the prince climbed in through the little window, Rapunzel was frightened. She had never seen anyone but the witch before.

"Do not be afraid," the prince told her gently. "I saw you at the window and thought you were so lovely that I had to come and see you!"

Rapunzel saw how fine and handsome the prince was, and her fear went away.

46

The prince visited Rapunzel many times after that. He brought her flowers, which she wove into garlands. While she wove, she sang songs to the prince in a sweet voice. Soon, the prince and Rapunzel fell in love with each other.

Then, one dreadful day, the witch learnt about the prince and his visits. Rapunzel told her by accident.

"You know," Rapunzel said, without thinking. "You pull on my hair much harder than the prince!"

"Prince! What prince?" the witch screamed. "You mean a prince has come here in secret? How dare you let him in!"

In a fury, the witch snatched up some scissors and cut off Rapunzel's long hair.

"You cannot let the prince into the tower now, my girl!" the witch cried in triumph. "Now, I will punish you for deceiving me."

The witch chanted a magic spell. At once, Rapunzel

found herself in a land far, far away from the tower, the forest and her handsome prince.

Meanwhile, the witch waited for the prince to come to the tower again. She heard him call: "Rapunzel! Rapunzel! Let down your hair!"

Holding Rapunzel's hair tightly in her hand, the witch let it down all the way to the ground. When the prince climbed up into the room, he got a frightful shock. Instead of his beautiful Rapunzel, an ugly old witch was waiting for him.

"I have punished Rapunzel for deceiving me," the witch screamed. "She is far away where you will never see her again. Now, I will punish you!"

With that, the witch leapt at the prince, ready to scratch his eyes out with her long nails. With a cry of alarm, the prince jumped out of the window to escape. Down, down, down he fell and landed in some briar bushes. The briar was full of thorns and they got into the prince's eyes. Suddenly, he found he could not see anything.

The prince was terribly unhappy. How could he find his beautiful Rapunzel now? For a long time, he wandered about in the forest, not knowing what to do. Then, he thought of a plan.

"I will ask everyone I meet if they have seen Rapunzel," he decided. "Someone must know where she is."

So, the prince wandered through the land asking about Rapunzel. He searched other lands, too, but nobody could tell him where she was. After several years, the poor blind prince had been all over the world seeking Rapunzel. But he could not find her.

One day, he was walking wearily along a road in a far distant land when he heard a sweet voice singing.

"It's Rapunzel! I have found her!" cried the prince.

It was indeed Rapunzel. She was sitting in the meadow close to her house, weaving flowers into a garland. As she wove, she sang, and as she sang, she thought of her prince and the happy days they had spent together long, long ago.

The prince called out her name. When Rapunzel heard it, she recognized it at once. She came running to him and flung her arms around his neck. She was crying with joy and kissing him, then crying again.

Rapunzel's tears fell into the prince's eyes and suddenly, he found he could see again.

"Darling Rapunzel!" he cried. "You are still so beautiful! I have found you once more and I shall never let you go again!"

Little Red Riding Hood

The wicked wolf was very hungry. He had not eaten for three whole days. He searched everywhere in the woods for food, but he could not find any. He was just starting to feel desperate when he saw a little girl. She was walking through the woods with a basket over her arm.

"Aha!" he said. "It's Little Red Riding Hood! She is a bit small, but she would make a good meal!"

The wolf's mouth began to water at the thought of food at last. He waited as Little Red Riding Hood came towards him. She was wearing a velvet cloak and a red hood which her mother had made for her.

"Good morning, Little Red Riding Hood," the wolf said with a smile. "Where are you going, my dear?"

Little Red Riding Hood was a bit frightened of the wolf, as her mother had told her never to talk to strangers. But the wolf seemed so friendly that she forgot her mother's warning.

"I am going to my grandmother who lives at the far end of the woods," she said. "She is not well, so I am taking her some cakes and butter."

"Dear me," said the wolf. "I am sorry your grandmother is not well. What a good girl you are to take her such nice food!"

As he spoke, the wicked wolf moved closer and closer to Little Red Riding Hood. Then, he saw some woodcutters at work among the trees not far away.

"I cannot eat Little Red Riding Hood while they are near," the wolf thought crossly. Then, he had an idea.

"I will go to visit your poor sick grandmother," he told Little Red Riding Hood. "I would like to cheer her up, poor old lady. I know," the wolf went on. "Let us have a race to your grandmother's house."

"All right," Little Red Riding Hood agreed.

"Good!" said the wolf. "You go that way, and I will go this way, and we shall see who gets there first! That will be fun, won't it?"

"Oh, yes!" Little Red Riding Hood agreed.

But the wicked wolf had given her the long way to her grandmother's house. He took a shorter way and got there long before she did.

"Who is there?" asked Little Red Riding Hood's grandmother as the wolf knocked rat-tat-tat on the door.

"It's me, Little Red Riding Hood," replied the wolf, speaking in a very high voice.

"In that case, come in. Just lift the latch and open the door," said the grandmother.

As soon as the wolf came into the room where she lay in bed, the grandmother gave a cry of alarm.

"But you are not . . ." she began. But before she could go any further, the wicked wolf opened his mouth, and swallowed her up in one go.

Quickly, the wolf put on one of the grandmother's nightdresses and her nightcap and spectacles. He jumped into bed and covered himself up. He was just in time. A moment later, there was a knock on the door — rat-tat-tat!

"Who is there?" called the wolf, making his voice high like grandmother's.

"It's me, Little Red Riding Hood!" came the reply.

"In that case," said the wolf, "Come in! Just lift the latch and open the door."

"I have brought you some cakes and butter, granny dear," said Little Red Riding Hood, as she came into the bedroom.

"How sweet of you, dear," the wolf replied. "Just put them down on the stool. Come here and sit by me!"

As Little Red Riding Hood came closer to the bed, she thought her grandmother looked a bit strange. She did not remember the old lady having big pointed ears or large hairy paws. Her eyes were so big too.

"Oh, granny," she said. "What big ears you have!"

"All the better to hear you with," said the wolf.

"And what big eyes you've got!"

"All the better to see you with!"

"And your hands – they are so large, and oh, goodness, what enormous teeth!" Little Red Riding Hood was becoming frightened now.

"All the better to hold you while I eat you!" cried the wolf, and he jumped out of bed. Before Little Red Riding Hood could get away, the wolf grabbed her, pushed her into his mouth and swallowed her in one go.

Now that the wolf had eaten Little Red Riding Hood and her grandmother, he felt very full indeed. He soon became drowsy and lay down on the bed. Before long, he was asleep and snoring very loudly.

Just then, a woodcutter came by the grandmother's cottage. "What a noise!" he thought. "I wonder if the old lady is all right?"

The woodcutter pushed open the cottage door and followed the sound of the snoring to the bedroom.

"That's not Little Red Riding Hood's granny!" he cried when he saw the wolf lying asleep on the bed. "And where is Little Red Riding Hood? Goodness, the wolf must have eaten both of them!"

Quickly, the woodcutter pulled his knife from his belt and cut the wolf open. To his surprise and relief, out jumped Little Red Riding Hood and her grandmother. They were both unhurt but very frightened.

"Oh my, how dark it was inside the wolf!" cried Little Red Riding Hood.

"Yes it was, dear!" her grandmother agreed. "What a terrible time we have had!"

Little Red Riding Hood was very grateful to the woodcutter for rescuing them.

"I will never talk to strangers in the woods ever again," she decided. "Specially if they are wolves!"

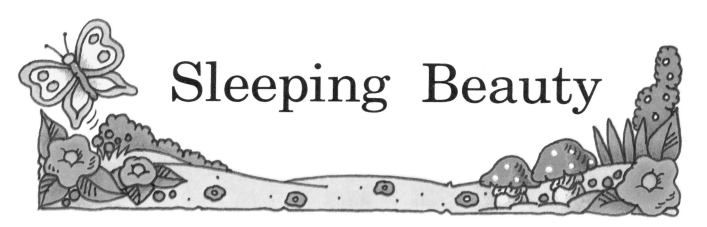

Sleeping Beauty

Fairy Carabosse was very angry. Because she was a very wicked fairy, terrible things happened when she was angry.

"So!" Carabosse said in a very threatening voice. "The King and Queen have a new baby daughter and they have not invited me to the christening! Well," Carabosse went on with an evil smile. "They will be very sorry!"

The wicked fairy got into her carriage, which was pulled by four big fat rats.

She drove very fast to the royal palace, where the King and Queen were giving a christening party for their baby daughter. Everyone gasped with fear when Fairy Carabosse burst into the great ballroom where the party was being held.

Before anyone could stop her, she marched up to the cradle where the princess, whose name was Aurora, lay sleeping.

"All important fairies bring presents to newly born princesses," Carabosse cackled wickedly. "I see the Fairy of the Crystal Fountain has given a garland of lilies. The Fairy of the Enchanted Meadow has given a bouquet of flowers. Well, I have a present, too!"

Carabosse looked round. Her black eyes gleamed in an evil way. She pointed a bony finger at the little princess. "My present is a curse!" she cried and the Queen shrieked in terror. "You will prick your finger on a spindle and you will die! That is the punishment for not inviting me to this party!"

With that, Fairy Carabosse left and drove away to the sound of great claps of thunder.

The Queen fainted. The King was weeping. His courtiers were wailing. Everyone was shocked at Fairy Carabosse's terrible curse.

Suddenly, a sweet, calm voice was heard.

"Do not worry," the voice said. "All will be well."

It was the Lilac Fairy, the most beautiful fairy of all. "All will be well," the Lilac Fairy said again. "I have not yet given my gift to the little princess."

The Lilac Fairy came close to the baby's cradle and smiled down at the child.

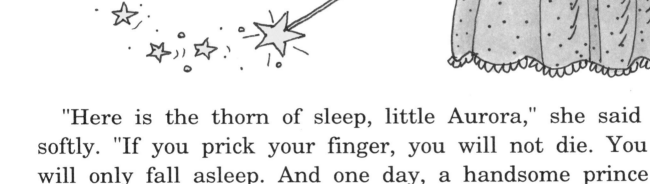

"Here is the thorn of sleep, little Aurora," she said softly. "If you prick your finger, you will not die. You will only fall asleep. And one day, a handsome prince will come along and wake you with a kiss."

The King was very grateful to the Lilac Fairy for her gift. Even so, he did not want to take any risks.

"If there are no spindles in the land," he said, "Aurora cannot prick her finger on any of them!"

So, the King ordered all the spindles in the land to be destroyed.

Many years passed and Princess Aurora grew into a very beautiful girl. On her sixteenth birthday, her parents gave a grand party for her. Lords and ladies from all over the country were invited.

Meanwhile, wicked Fairy Carabosse was getting

impatient. She wanted her curse to come true.

"Sixteen years!" Carabosse said. "It is long enough!"

Carabosse had not destroyed her spindle when the King gave his order. Instead, she had hidden it away. Now, she took it from its hiding place and hid it again, but this time in a bunch of roses. Then, Carabosse went to Aurora's birthday party in disguise.

"Here is a fine birthday gift for you, my dear," Carabosse told the princess.

"Roses! Oh, how beautiful they are," Aurora cried, but as soon as she took the roses in her hands, the hidden spindle pricked her finger.

At once, the princess fell down in a deep sleep. Nothing anyone could do could wake her up. So, sorrowfully, the King ordered the princess to be placed on a velvet couch. There she slept and looked so lovely that people called her Sleeping Beauty.

When the Lilac Fairy heard what had happened, she flew straight away to the royal palace.

"I cannot break the spell, I fear," the Lilac Fairy told the grieving King and Queen. "But I can protect Aurora and everyone in the palace. Then you will be safe until the handsome prince arrives. It may take a long time."

So, the Lilac Fairy touched everyone in the palace with her wand and they all fell asleep at once, just like Princess Aurora. A great mass of bushes and thorns grew up around the palace. It became completely hidden and as time passed, many people forgot it was there.

The Lilac Fairy stayed close by. She was watching out for a handsome prince who would wake Aurora with a kiss and so break the spell. Fifty years went by, then a hundred, but no prince came. Then, one day, a prince from a faraway country arrived to hunt wild boar in the woods near the palace. His name was Desire, but people called him Prince Charming because he was so handsome and gracious.

"At last!" said the Lilac Fairy when she saw him.

Prince Charming sat down by a stream to rest for a while. Suddenly, he saw the Lilac Fairy floating along in a little boat drawn by three giant butterflies. She stepped ashore and sat down beside him.

"Have you heard about Sleeping Beauty and the enchanted palace where time stands still?" she asked the prince.

"Why no!" he replied. "Is the palace near here? I should like to see it."

"Very near," said the Lilac Fairy and she told him all about Princess Aurora and what had happened to her.

The prince was very interested. "I must see her," he said. "Take me to her at once!"

The Lilac Fairy waved her magic wand and the bushes and thorns which had grown up around the palace disappeared. Then, she led the prince into the palace to the room where Aurora lay on her velvet couch, still sleeping.

"Oh, she is beautiful!" Prince Charming said. "I have only just seen her, but I love her already."

"Wake her up, then!" the Lilac Fairy told him.

The prince bent down and kissed Aurora on the lips. At once, her eyes opened and as soon as she saw the handsome Prince Charming, she fell in love with him.

The Lilac Fairy waved her magic wand again and everyone in the palace woke up. The King and Queen were overjoyed to see their daughter again, and that same day, Aurora and Prince Charming were married. Afterwards, they left for their honeymoon and sailed away down the stream in the Lilac Fairy's boat, drawn by three giant butterflies.

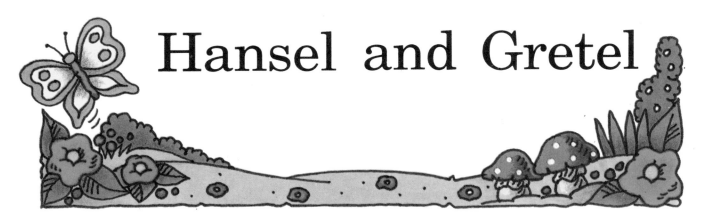

Hansel and Gretel

Hansel and Gretel were very frightened. Their father and mother had left them in a forest glade hours ago. Now, it was growing dark.

"Where are they?" said Gretel, crying. "Why haven't they come back for us?"

Hansel tried to comfort his sister. "I don't know," he said. "But father said we should wait here in the glade while he and mother went to collect some brushwood. So we must not wander off, or they will never find us."

What Hansel did not know was that his father and mother were not coming back. They had gone home to their cottage on the edge of the forest.

"Oh dear, oh dear!" said mother. "I do hope Hansel and Gretel are all right . . . there are all kinds of dangers in the forest!"

"Do not worry," father told her. "The children will come to no harm. We had to leave them in the forest because we have no food for them here. Some kind person will find them and take care of them, you will see!"

"Oh dear!" mother said. "I do hope you are right!"

By this time, it was night in the forest. Hansel and Gretel were cold and hungry as well as frightened. They were also very tired. At last they fell asleep beneath a big oak tree with their arms around each other.

Next morning, they awoke just as rays of sunlight lit up the forest. They could hear a bird singing. He was a chirpy little bluebird perched on a branch above their heads.

"I wonder if he knows which is the path to our home?" said Gretel.

"I know where there is a cottage," the bird said. "Follow me."

The bird did not fly away out of sight among the trees. Instead, it flew in front of Hansel and Gretel and led them along the pathways through the forest until they came to a cottage in a glade. As Hansel and Gretel came close to the cottage, they could smell something very sweet.

"It's the cottage, Hansel!" Gretel cried. "Look, it's made of gingerbread! The windows are made of sugar!"

Gretel was right. Even the fence around the cottage was made of gingerbread. The fence was decorated with little cut-out figures of animals.

Hansel and Gretel were so hungry that they started eating pieces of the walls and windows.

As they ate, they did not see a witch come out of the front door. The witch was very ugly. She had a long nose with a pair of glasses, because she was short-sighted and could not see very well.

Even so, she knew Hansel and Gretel were there, because she could smell them.

Suddenly the children heard the witch cry:

"Whicky, whacky, snackerty-poo!" She waved a juniper branch in the air, and Hansel and Gretel found they could not move. The witch had cast a spell on them.

"Now, I've got you!" the witch cackled.

She threw a rope around Hansel's neck and started to poke him with her bony fingers.

"Too thin, much too thin!" she muttered. She waved the juniper bough, said the magic words backwards and freed Gretel from the spell.

"Fetch me some water!" the witch ordered Gretel. "I'll make a nice vegetable stew for your brother. He needs to be fattened up!"

The stew was only the first of many big meals that Hansel had to eat. The witch put him in a cage and made him eat so much that before long, he grew very fat. The witch could not see this because of her bad eyesight. So, every morning, she told Hansel to poke his fingers through the bars of the cage.

"Show me how fat you are!" she demanded. Hansel knew she wanted him to be fat so she could eat him. So, to fool her, he poked a twig through the bars.

"Hmmmm, still too skinny!" muttered the witch, as she felt the twig.

After a few weeks, though, the witch became impatient. "Fat or skinny, I'm going to eat him!" she cried. "Gretel! Look inside the oven and see that it is ready for baking!"

Gretel was afraid. How could she save Hansel and herself? For the witch meant to eat Gretel, too.

"I know," Gretel thought. "I'll pretend I don't understand." So, she called to the witch: "But I don't know how an oven should be when it is ready — please show me!"

"How stupid the girl is!" muttered the witch. "It's easy — look, like this..."

The witch bent over the oven and put out her hands to feel the heat. Quickly, Gretel rushed up and gave her a tremendous push. With a terrible shriek, the witch fell into the oven, head first. Gretel banged the door shut.

Gretel ran over to the cage and let Hansel out. They

danced around and around. "The wicked witch is dead!" they cried.

Suddenly all round the cottage, the figures of animals along the fence began to come to life.

"The witch baked us into gingerbread," they told Hansel and Gretel. "Now, thanks to you, we are free!"

Hansel and Gretel wanted to go home to their father and mother as quickly as they could. But first they searched the witch's cottage. They found huge chests full of gold and jewels. They filled two sacks with the treasure, and then they saw the little bluebird. It had come back to lead them home. Their parents cried with joy to see their children safe.

"Look at all this treasure!" they cried when Hansel and Gretel emptied the sacks on the table. "Now we can buy all the food we want! We shall never be hungry again!"

The Emperor's New Clothes

The Emperor cried: "Are you telling me that you can make a cloth that is invisible?"

"Why, yes sire!" replied one of the two tailors who had just arrived at the Emperor's court.

"Only clever people can see this magic cloth. Foolish people cannot!" the other tailor said.

"This is marvellous!" the Emperor thought. "If I wear a suit made of this cloth, then I will know which of my courtiers are clever and which are fools."

The Emperor was very fond of clothes. He loved dressing up and often wore several different outfits every day. But invisible cloth! That was something he had never heard of before.

"I must have it!" he decided.

The Emperor never dreamed that the two tailors were not tailors at all. They were rascals who were playing a trick on him.

"Start making this magic cloth at once!" the Emperor commanded, and gave the two rascals a large amount of money.

The two men were delighted, of course.

"How stupid this Emperor is to believe a story like that!" they told each other, laughing.

They set up looms, machines for weaving cloth. They ordered the best silk and gold thread to weave the cloth and pretended to start work.

Before long, the whole town was talking about the magic invisible cloth. Everyone wanted to have some. The two rascals seemed to be very busy and for many days, people could hear them working away at their looms. The truth was, though, that the two were doing nothing at all. They were just making noises that sounded like looms working.

After a while the Emperor wanted to know how the magic cloth was getting on. So, he sent one of his ministers to visit the two men. They welcomed the minister into their house and showed him their looms.

"Here is the cloth, sir!" they said, pointing to the looms. "We hope you like it, is it not very beautiful?"

The minister stared at the loom. There was no cloth on it. "I cannot see anything," he thought. "Oh, dear! Foolish people cannot see this cloth, can they? I must be foolish, then." This worried the minister very much. "No one must know this," he decided.

So, he pretended to admire the cloth he could not see. "Why, it's marvellous, wonderful!" he cried. "What lovely colours! What beautiful patterns! I must tell the Emperor about it straight away."

The two rascals tried hard not to laugh as the minister rushed off to the palace with the great news.

A little while later, the Emperor and his courtiers came to see the cloth on the looms. The two rascals bowed low before the Emperor.

"Sire, we are very honoured by your visit," they said.

They showed the Emperor the looms. They were empty of course. There was not a single thread on them. Like the minister before him, the Emperor thought:

"I cannot see anything! Oh, my, does this mean I am a fool? No one must know this."

"Why, the cloth is splendid!" the Emperor cried. "I have never seen such beautiful cloth in my whole life!"

Everyone agreed with him of course. The courtiers could not see any cloth on the loom, either, but no one wanted to be thought foolish.

"Sire!" the courtiers told him. "You must have a suit made from this wonderful cloth. You can wear it at the Grand Parade!"

The Emperor became excited. "Yes, yes, of course I can!" he cried. "This is wonderful! You two have done me a great service," he told the two rascals. "I will make both of you Knights of the Garter! You will have the title of Tailors to the Emperor!"

The night before the Grand Parade, the two rascals sat up all night, pretending to sew the magic cloth into a splendid new suit for the Emperor. Then, they sent a message to the palace to say the suit was finished.

Next morning, the Emperor arrived to try on his new clothes. He undressed and the two rascals pretended to put the suit on him. "You cannot feel you are wearing it, sire!" they told him. "The cloth is as light and fine as a cobweb."

The Emperor looked at his reflection in a mirror. He turned this way and that, pretending to admire his new

clothes. Of course, he could see no clothes at all, but he said he was delighted. His courtiers seemed pleased, too.

"What a wonderful suit!" they exclaimed. "How well it fits! What a marvellous style!"

The Grand Parade was a great success. The Emperor walked proudly through the street in his new suit. The crowds marvelled at it. "Isn't it great!" they said. "Isn't it grand?"

No one dared admit, of course, that the Emperor was not wearing any clothes at all. For fear of being thought foolish, everyone pretended to admire his new outfit.

But there was one person who did not. A child was watching the parade pass by. "Why, the Emperor isn't wearing any clothes at all!" the child cried. "He's quite naked!"

At this, the crowd stopped cheering. Everyone looked at the child in horror.

"But it's true!" the child insisted. "Look, the Emperor is naked!"

The Emperor went very red in the face. He knew the child was telling the truth, and so did everyone else in the town. But everyone, except the child, was too proud to admit it.

The Emperor finished the parade as quickly as he could and rushed back to the palace. He knew now that he was indeed a fool. For only a fool pretends to see what he does not see.

Pinocchio

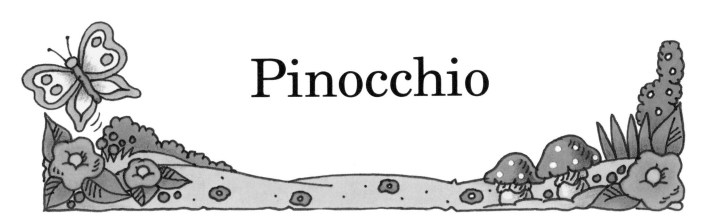

G eppetto the carpenter said: "Oh dear, where is Pinocchio? He has been nothing but trouble since the day I made him."

Pinocchio was a puppet and a very naughty one. He was rude and disobedient and lazy. When Geppetto sent him to school, he went off to see a Punch and Judy show instead.

Now, Pinocchio had gone out, and hours later he had not yet come home. Even though Pinocchio gave him a lot of trouble, Geppetto loved him and he was very worried that something bad had happened to him.

Hours passed. Still, Pinocchio did not come home. At last, Geppetto could wait no longer. He locked up his workshop and began searching for Pinocchio in the town. He searched everywhere throughout the land, but Pinocchio was nowhere to be found. So, Geppetto got a small boat and sailed out to sea. Maybe he would find Pinocchio there.

Some fishermen warned Geppetto that the sea was dangerous, but the carpenter would not listen.

"The old man will surely drown," the fishermen said sadly.

Where was Pinocchio?

The naughty puppet had gone to a faraway place called Playland. In Playland, the children played games all day long. No one went to school. No one read books or did lessons. It was marvellous.

Then, one day, Pinocchio got a terrible fright. He looked in the mirror and saw he had grown two big ears like a donkey's. His face was growing furry and his nose was changing into a flat snout.

"I'm turning into a donkey!" Pinocchio cried. "Help me, somebody, help me!"

But there was no one to help Pinocchio. The others had all turned into donkeys, too. They were sold to farmers and other people who used donkeys for work.

The farmer who bought Pinocchio was very cruel. He whipped him and did not give him enough to eat. One day, Pinocchio fell and hurt his hind leg. Afterwards, he could not walk properly.

"This donkey is no use to me now," said the farmer. So, he threw Pinocchio into the sea, and left him to drown. Just as Pinocchio was struggling in the water trying not to sink, he saw a blue light coming towards him. It was a beautiful lady.

"I am the Blue Fairy, your fairy godmother," the lady said. "I have come to save you."

She waved her magic wand and at once Pinocchio turned into a puppet again. Because he was made of wood, he floated easily on the water.

"Oh, thank you, thank you!" Pinocchio cried. "Now I shall not drown."

It was the first time Pinocchio had said "Thank you" to anyone.

"How did you become a donkey, Pinocchio?" the Blue Fairy asked.

Pinocchio felt ashamed, so he told a lie.

"I don't know," he replied. As soon as he spoke, his nose grew four inches longer.

"Yes, you do. You ran away to Playland, didn't you?" said the Blue Fairy.

"No, I didn't! Someone forced me to go there. I didn't want to go!" Suddenly, Pinocchio's nose grew another four inches.

"Are you telling me the truth?" asked the Blue Fairy.

"Yes! Of course I am!" Pinocchio lied. His nose grew another four inches. By this time, it was almost as long as his arm. "This is terrible," Pinocchio thought. "It is worse than being turned into a donkey."

"If you tell me another lie, your nose will grow longer again!" the Blue Fairy warned him. "You have been naughty, disobedient and lazy. You have given your father Geppetto a lot of worry. That is the truth, isn't it?"

Pinocchio felt very ashamed.

"Yes, all you say is true," he confessed.

As soon as Pinocchio told the truth, his nose became its proper size again.

"That's better," said the Blue Fairy. "Be good from now on and always tell the truth. Then one day you might become real."

"Oh, I would like that very much!" Pinocchio said excitedly. "I will go home to my father now and be very good to him."

The Blue Fairy looked sad.

"You cannot go home to your father," she told Pinocchio. "He went looking for you out at sea and has not been seen again."

"You mean he is lost?" Pinocchio said. "Then I must find him!"

At once, Pinocchio started swimming. He swam all over the sea, searching for Geppetto. Before long he became very tired and fell asleep, floating in the water.

Suddenly, a huge whale came along and sucked Pinocchio into its mouth. Pinocchio found himself tumbling down the whale's throat, and into its stomach.

To his surprise, someone else was there. It was Geppetto. "Father!" Pinocchio cried. "I am so glad to see you again. How did you get here?"

"The same way as you," Geppetto said. "The whale swallowed me."

"Well, I have come to save you, father!"

"How can you do that?" Geppetto wanted to know.

"We can swim out!" said Pinocchio.

"But I cannot swim."

"Then get on my back, Father, and I will do the swimming," Pinocchio told him.

With Geppetto on his back, Pinocchio swam up the whale's throat and into its huge mouth. Suddenly, the whale gave a tremendous sneeze. Its mouth opened and Pinocchio and Geppetto shot out like a rocket.

"You have saved both of us, Pinocchio!" Geppetto said joyfully.

From then on, Pinocchio lived happily with Geppetto at home. He went to school and learned his lessons and Geppetto became very proud of him.

One morning, Pinocchio got a wonderful surprise. He looked in the mirror and saw that he was no longer a wooden puppet.

"I'm real! I'm real!" he shouted, jumping up and down with excitement.

"That is because you are good and work hard," Geppetto told him.

Rip Van Winkle

Rip Van Winkle often went to the mountains with his dog Wolf. He was going hunting and he promised to bring home plenty of food for his family. But Rip Van Winkle had another reason for escaping into the mountains. He wanted to get away from his wife. Mrs Van Winkle used to nag him because he did not work hard enough on his farm.

"The apples in the orchard need picking! The milk must be taken to market! The chickens have to be fed . . . the roof needs mending . . ." Mrs Van Winkle went on and on. "And what do you do all day? You play games with the children, and sit in the inn talking to your friends! I'm sorry I married you, Rip Van Winkle! I should never have fallen for your blue eyes!"

"I'm sorry I married you, too," Rip Van Winkle thought, but he did not dare say so out loud. His wife would start shouting at him again.

So, instead, Rip Van Winkle escaped to the mountains where it was peaceful and calm. He took his gun with him, but instead of hunting he lay on the grass with his dog Wolf beside him and watched the sky. Rip Van Winkle could spend many hours like this.

Then, one day, he saw a group of travellers on the mountainside. Rip Van Winkle was surprised because he had never seen any of them before.

"I thought I knew everyone in the villages near the mountains," Rip muttered to himself. "What strange clothes they are wearing. People used to dress like that two hundred years ago!"

Rip Van Winkle went a bit closer to get a better look. One of the men saw him. "Hello there!" he called out in a friendly voice. "Come and join us. We are having a party!"

Rip saw that the men were playing skittles. He loved skittles, so he accepted the invitation.

"Have a drink, friend," said one of the men. He held out a tankard of wine. Rip took it and drank a little. The wine tasted very old, but Rip liked it. He drank some more and sat down.

Close to, the men looked even stranger than before. Their leader wore a big loaf-shaped hat with a big red feather in it. All the men had long, full beards.

"No one wears a beard like that any more," thought Rip Van Winkle. "How very odd."

Rip Van Winkle played a few games of skittles and drank some more wine. Then, suddenly he remembered where he had seen these men before. "They look like the people in that old painting in the village inn!" he said to himself.

He was not very sure about it, though, because by now, he had drunk too much wine and felt very drowsy.

Before long, Rip Van Winkle fell asleep. When he woke up, the strange men were gone. Rip's dog Wolf was nowhere to be seen. His gun, which he had put down beside him, was just a heap of rusty metal and rotten wood. Then, Rip realized that his beard had grown very long and white. When he stood up, it reached down to his feet. And his clothes were full of holes and tears!

"Oh dear! What will my wife say if I go home looking like this?" Rip Van Winkle cried.

Even so, he had to go home. There was nowhere else to go. So, Rip Van Winkle threw his long white beard over his shoulder and walked back down the mountainside.

When he reached the village where he lived, he got a big shock.

"It's completely different!" he said to himself. "I don't remember it like this. Those houses were not there before! And where is the village inn?"

Where the inn had once stood, there was a big hotel. Rip Van Winkle did not know anyone he saw in the street.

Everyone stared at him, though. He looked very odd in his torn clothes and long beard. Just then, a baby began to cry. It was frightened by Rip Van Winkle and his strange appearance.

"Hush now, little Rip," the baby's mother said. "The old man won't hurt you."

"Did you call him Rip?" Rip Van Winkle wanted to know.

"Yes, that's his name," the mother replied. "He is named after my father, who disappeared in the mountains twenty years ago."

"Twenty years ago! Did I sleep for twenty years?" Rip Van Winkle thought. "How is that possible?"

"What is your name?" he asked the mother.

"Judith," she told him.

"Judith!" Rip Van Winkle cried. "I had a daughter called Judith, but she was only three when I went for a walk in the mountains! How old are you?"

"Twenty-three," Judith said.

"This is my daughter, all grown up," Rip Van Winkle thought, astonished. "So, I DID sleep for twenty years."

"Judith!" he cried out loud. "Don't you know me? I am your father, Rip Van Winkle!"

Judith looked at him, puzzled. Then, she saw how blue his eyes were. Only her father had eyes like that.

"Father, you've come back!" Judith cried and flung her arms around his neck.

Now, everyone was crowding round, wanting to know what Rip had been doing for twenty years. But there was one thing Rip wanted to know.

"Where is my wife, Mrs Van Winkle?" he asked.

"Oh, she died some time ago," an old woman told him. "She got in a terrible temper one day, and gave herself a heart attack!"

Rip Van Winkle felt sorry, but thankful at the same time. Mrs Van Winkle would never nag him again.

That evening, the whole village held a party to welcome Rip Van Winkle home. There was plenty of food and wine and games of skittles. Rip had lots of food and had several games of skittles, but he did not drink the wine.

"I am having too much fun!" he thought. "If I drink wine I might fall asleep for twenty years again. I am enjoying myself too much for that!"